I0771414

Springer Literary House LLC
6260 Lavender Cloud Place
Las Vegas, Nevada 89122, USA

www.springerliteraryhouse.com

DAILY ROUTINES THAT MAKE YOU LAUGH

Poetic Rhymes from Everyday Life

My Life's Poetry Collection: Volume 1

ACKNOWLEDGMENT

Creating **Daily Routines That Make You Laugh: Poetic Rhymes from Everyday Life** has been a joyful and fulfilling journey, one filled with smiles, quiet reflections, and moments of inspiration drawn from the everyday.

To my family and friends, thank you for being the heart behind many of these poems. Your presence, laughter, and support have shaped this collection in countless ways.

A special thank-you to Emily Blake, my editor, for your keen eye, patience, and thoughtful feedback. Your editing brought clarity and life to every page.

To Springer Literary House LLC, my publisher, thank you for believing in my work and guiding it from manuscript to published book. Your professionalism and encouragement made this dream a reality.

To Aleksei Chorabelsky, thank you for your invaluable help with formatting and publishing. Your attention to detail and dedication ensured everything came together beautifully.

And to you, dear reader, thank you for opening these pages. May the rhymes within bring a smile to your face and remind you that humor and poetry exist even in the simplest routines of life.

With heartfelt gratitude.

REY SAÑOSA

TABLE OF CONTENTS

Introduction

Welcome to ***Daily Routines That Make You Laugh: Poetic Rhymes from Everyday Life***, a playful collection of short rhyming poems inspired by the hilarious mess found in everyday routines: from coffee catastrophes to tech disasters, parenting puzzles to grocery store gymnastics. These tiny poems prove that life's biggest headaches sometimes come wrapped in socks missing their partners and that laughter is basically free therapy (no appointments needed). So buckle up, grab your coffee (if it's still in the cup), and get ready for some "Wait, that happened to me?!" moments.

Chapter 1

Morning Madness

A fun and relatable take on the whirlwind of daily morning routines: alarm clocks, lost socks, spilled coffee, and the race against time.

These rhymes capture the chaos, charm, and comedy of starting the day.

Morning Mess

I spilled my coffee on my shirt,

Then stubbed my toe, oh! how it hurt.

I missed the bus by half a mile,

Showed up late with half a smile.

Life's not perfect, that's okay,

Just laugh it off and start your day.

Cereal Catastrophe

Poured the milk before the flakes,

Rookie move, for goodness' sake!

The box was empty, I had no clue!

Guess the kids were snacking too.

Used a fork, no spoon in sight,

Breakfast just won't start right.

Toothpaste Trouble

Squeezed too hard, it hit the floor,

Bounced and slid right out the door.

Brushed my sleeve instead of teeth,

Now I smell like mint beneath.

Mirror's fogged, the sink's a mess,

Morning wins, I must confess.

The Alarm Betrayal

Hit snooze once more, or maybe ten,

Then dreamt I ruled a lime-green den.

Woke up late, no socks in sight,

Brushed my teeth with all my might.

Set alarms? Yeah, that's the trick,

Don't trust them when you sleep too quick.

Forgetful Frenzy

Keys, phone, wallet, where'd they go?

Lost again, I'm moving slow.

Check the fridge? Nope, just last place,

Jacket pockets, a wild goose chase.

Forgetful days make you sigh,

But laughing's cheaper than to cry.

Sock Mystery

I swear I had a matching pair,

But now one sock is just not there.

Checked the washer, looked around,

That sneaky sock can't be found.

So I'll work with mismatched sock,

Honestly, who's gonna clock?

Mirror Talk

Looked in the mirror, saw a zit,

It popped up fast, now I'm unfit.

I smiled, I posed, tried not to freak,

Filters make me flawless, at least for a week.

Don't let flaws define your grace,

A real smile wins the beauty race.

Overthinker's Night

Lying in bed to count some sheep,

Instead, I questioned life too deep.

Did I offend that guy at lunch?

Why did I text 'ok' too much?

At 2 a.m., my brain's a wreck,

Guess I'll just scroll and double-check.

CHAPTER 2

HOUSEHOLD HIJINKS

A lighthearted look at the everyday chaos, quirks, and comical moments that unfold within the walls of home.

From laundry mishaps to kitchen catastrophes, these playful rhymes celebrate the humor hidden in household routines.

Socks on the Loose

Another sock has gone AWOL,

Vanished from its laundry hole.

Left behind, just one to wear,

Fashion's gamble, bold and rare.

If your pair is never found,

Rock mismatched, it's quite profound.

Kids' Toy Trap

I walked at night, the house calm and neat,

Till LEGO attacked my poor bare feet.

I screamed so loud, I scared the cat,

My dignity went flat, just like that.

Tiny bricks with ninja force,

Watch your step or curse the course.

The Haircut Hiccup

Tried to trim my fringe last night,

Now it looks like a crime scene's in sight.

Now my bangs are way too short,

My mirror filed a police report.

DIY is sometimes bold,

But some things need a pro to hold.

The Missing Remote

The couch has swallowed it again,

The remote's gone rogue, perhaps to Spain.

I flip each cushion, beg and plead,

Still stuck on "Kids Channel," oh, the need!

If life won't change with just one click,

Time to get up, no more Netflix.

Chapter 3

Work & Tech Woes

From never-ending emails to glitchy gadgets, this section dives into the frustrations and funny moments of modern work life.

Whether it's Zoom fails or printer tantrums, these rhymes capture the daily grind with a digital twist.

Pajama Panic

Logged in for Zoom, still in my pajamas,

Hair all wild like haunted dramas.

Turned off the cam, but the mic was live,

They heard me sing "Staying Alive."

Embarrassed? Yep, but here's the deal,

Laugh it off and keep it real.

Monday Mood

Coffee brewed, but where's the zip?

Feels like time took a weekend trip.

Emails scream and meetings moan,

Brain still stuck in Sunday zone.

But friend, don't lose your chill today,

Just think, Friday's coming, it's on its way.

Email Overload

Inbox full, a never-ending scroll,

Emails pile and take their toll.

Reply to one, ten more appear,

"Urgent" flags scream, oh! the fear.

Best advice when work's a flood?

Breathe deep, then tackle one email, bud.

Wi-Fi Woes

Internet dies mid Zoom debate,

Frozen faces just won't wait.

Restart the router and offer a dance,

Pray the signal gets a chance.

When Wi-Fi fails and nerves go fried,

Just laugh it off, then Netflix, glide.

.

Meeting Marathon

Meetings stack like bricks on bricks,

Talking 'round the clock with no quick fix.

Notes are lost, ideas delayed,

Coffee fuels the masquerade.

If meetings last the whole dang day,

Just doodle, dream, or sneak away.

Keyboard Catastrophe

Spilled my drink on keys today,

Letters drowned and ran away.

Typing now is slow and sticky,

Sticky keys make work less tricky.

If tech fails, don't curse or swear,

Clean it up or just declare, "Repair!"

Printer Panic

Paper jammed, the printer moans,

Flashing lights like warning tones.

Staples stuck and ink runs dry,

That urgent print? Just say goodbye.

Old techs got a stubborn streak,

Patience wins, but so does sneak.

Lost in Translation

Typed a text with auto-check,

Sent a message, what the heck?

Said "I love you" turned to "I lob stew,"

Now they're wondering what to do.

Tech's a friend who likes to play,

Proofread twice or send astray.

Social Media Spiral

Scrolling feeds for just a bit,

Two hours gone, now I admit.

Likes and comments fill my brain,

But real-life calls to break the chain.

Balance screens with real-life fun,

Or your days completely done.

The Forgotten Password

Password lost, can't get in,

"Try again," said with a grin.

Reset links and secret clues,

Logging in is quite the ruse.

Passwords many, memories few,

Keep them safe, or bid adieu.

Deadline Dash

Deadline looming, stress is high,

Brain fog thick, no time to sigh.

Typing fast with coffee shots,

Dodging typos, losing plots.

Deadlines teach a tough respect,

Plan ahead, and you'll deflect.

Office Snack Thief

Cookies gone from breakroom shelf,

Was it, Bob? Or just myself?

Office snacks cause mystery,

Sharing builds the history.

Snack with friends or eat alone,

Either way, don't take the throne.

Email Etiquette

"Per my last email," tone so cold,

Writing nicely is often bold.

Polite words can smooth the way,

Work emails save the day.

Words can wound or words can mend,

So, CC Karma in the end.

Reply All Regret

Meant to send it just to Jane,

Now the whole team is in my lane.

GIFs and jokes and private sass,

Oops! It's HR on my class.

Next time, breathe and check that line,

Reply All's a steep decline.

Cubicle Life

Walls are so small, but thoughts run wide,

Daydreams break the workday tide.

Sticky notes and desk décor,

Make this box feel something more.

Corner nook or cubicle cave,

We make it ours and slightly brave.

Office Fashion Fiasco

Blazer sharp or hoodie bold,

Fashion rules? They're kinda old.

Flip-flops squeak down marble halls,

Ties too tight? We take the falls.

Wear what makes you feel brand-new,

Confidence is your best shoe.

The Promotion Dream

I work, I slay, I bring the flair,

Still no crown? Do they even care?

Smiled through chaos, nailed each task,

Where's my raise? Is that too much to ask?

Hold your fire, but don't play small,

You were made to stand up tall.

Friday Freedom

Last hour ticks, and spirits soar,

Fun plans and so much more.

Wrap it up, the week's complete,

Weekend joys can't be beat.

Inbox closed, we hit delete,

Goodbye stress and office seat.

Chapter 4

Parenting & Family Fiascos

A humorous and honest peek into the beautiful chaos of family life.

From toddler tantrums to sibling squabbles and unforgettable parenting moments, these rhymes celebrate the love, laughter, and little disasters that make family truly unforgettable.

Morning Mayhem

Kids are all yelling, doors go slam,

Where's my shoe? Who ate that ham?

Breakfast chaos, socks don't match,

Trying hard to stay attached.

Parenting's a wild ride,

But love's the compass by our side.

Homework Helper

Math sheets make me want to cry,

Why's the answer always 'pi'?

Patience tested, brains may melt,

Cheating? Nope, I've always felt.

Numbers dance, my brains on fire,

Calculator might expire.

Toy Turf War

"Mine!" "No, mine!" the battle cry,

Toys and toys are flying high.

Mediator in between,

Keeping peace behind the scene.

Sibling love grows through the fight,

Turn the noise into delight.

The Lost Toy

Teddy vanished, panic grows,

Under couch or where no one knows?

Search the house, retrace the trail,

Found it stuck inside a pail.

Lost and found, the game we play,

Toys hide smart, but not all day.

School Run Race

Drive through traffic, dodge and weave,

Shoes half on, we race to leave.

Late again? Just shrug and grin,

Chaos means the day begins.

Horns are honking, backpacks fly,

Gold star just for getting by.

Family Dinner Drama

Veggies launched across the plate,

Dog's on guard, it's dinner fate.

"Try one bite!" becomes a chant,

"No, I can't, I really can't!"

Still, we laugh and share the feast,

Love's the main course, not the least.

Parent Tech Support

"Mom, my screen just froze again!"
"Dad, the Wi-Fi's gone, insane!"
Tiny cries, big tech despair,
Panicked kids, wild-clicking flair.
Parents Google, kids just know,
Family fixes, tech in tow.

Proud Moments

First steps, first words, day well won,

Tiny triumphs, second to none.

Celebrate each sweet success,

Moments filled with happiness.

Family's heartbeat, strong and near,

Love grows deeper every year.

Toddler Takeover

The kids are asleep, the house is still,

A peaceful pause until the shrill.

A toy drops, a door goes bang,

Peace was shattered by a toddler gang.

Parenting's full of noise and fun,

Survive the chaos, a new day has just begun.

The Lost Lunchbox

Lunchbox gone, now where'd it go?

Fridge? Backpack? I just don't know.

Found it later in the car,

On secret travels, near and far.

Kids may lose things throughout the day,

But love, like lunch, won't drift away.

Bedtime Bargain

Five more minutes, make it ten!

They strike the deal, then stall again.

Stories, hugs, and water sips,

Negotiations from tiny lips.

It drains your night, in pajama power,

But love still blooms like a midnight flower.

Family Selfie Fumble

Posed for a photo, smiles bright,

Blinking, blinking, not quite right.

Phones go off, or someone sneezes,

Perfect shot just teases.

Family pictures, a mess of fun,

Laugh it off when all is done.

Chapter 5

Errands & Everyday Tasks

From grocery runs to laundry loads, this section highlights the humor in the ordinary.

These rhymes turn to-do lists into tales, proving that even the most mundane moments can bring a smile or a sigh.

Grocery Gambit

List in hand, I hit the store,

Forgot the list, I'm doomed once more.

Wandering aisles, what did I seek?

Bought three snacks, but not the meat.

Grocery runs are hit or miss,

Next time, maybe text the list.

The Parking Spot

Circle 'round for what feels like hours,

All spots are claimed by shopping powers.

Finally snag one far away,

Carry bags like it's a relay.

Some take time, and that's okay,

Finding a spot can make your day.

Laundry Mount

Clothes pile high like Everest,

Socks were lost in this tangled quest.

Wash, dry, fold, repeat the grind,

Laundry's trap that steals your mind.

But fresh and folded, neat and sweet,

Until it screams, "Surprise! Repeat.

The DIY Disaster

Bought a shelf to build today,

Instructions lost, what can I say?

Screws went missing, boards went smack,

Now it leans like it's about to crack.

DIY is brave and bold,

But sometimes best left to the old.

Chapter 6

Food & Drink Follies

A tasty collection of rhymes celebrating kitchen chaos, mealtime mishaps, and the little joys of eating and sipping.

From burnt toast to spilled coffee, these poems serve up the lighter side of life's culinary adventures.

The Late-Night Snack

Fridge light glows, temptation calls,

Cookies, cheese, and midnight brawls.

Calories lost in late-night glee,

Tomorrow's diet? We'll just see.

Tomorrow's diet? Yeah, right, I crack,

For now, I'm king of the midnight snack.

Fridge Surprise

Opened the fridge, oh! what a smell!

Like something died and said farewell.

A veggie rotted, lost the fight,

Now it's a blob from the science site.

Ignore it? Nope, that's not the way,

Or you'll have a lab experiment someday.

Burnt Toast Blues

Toast popped up with blackened face,

Smoke alarms join the race.

Coffee saved the morning mood,

Though breakfast was less than good.

Not every day is flawless bright,

Some days start with burnt delight.

Recipe Roulette

Tried a recipe, followed each line,

Ended up with something not quite fine.

Salt too much, sugar too low,

Dinner tasted like a show.

Cooking's fun until it's a mess,

Then call for pizza, no need to stress.

Coffee Crisis

Ran out of beans, no coffee cup,

Morning without? I want to give up!

Caffeine is the fuel I need,

Without it, my brain won't proceed.

Keep stocked up, don't let it lapse,

Or mornings turn into mishaps.

Leftovers Logic

Leftovers piled, a Tupperware tower,

In the fridge, they plot their power.

Will it spoil? Should I eat?

Guessing games with frozen meat.

Waste not, want not is wise,

But sometimes science tells lies.

Dining Out Drama

Restaurant food, fancy and fine,

Waiter spills a glass of wine.

Stains on shirts, a startled stare,

Laugh it off, just don't despair.

Dining out's a fun surprise,

Even when it's not so wise.

The Snack Attack

At 2 p.m., my tummy cried,

"Just one small snack!" I boldly lied.

I raided chips, then cookies too,

Even ate old mystery goo.

Snack time wins with zero shame,

The crumbs will take the blame.

Takeout Temptation

Scroll menu for hours long,

Craving food that feels so wrong.

Takeout's here, pizza and fries,

No pots, no pans, no messy tries.

Sometimes, quick beats all the rest,

Treat yourself, you deserve the best.

Kitchen Dance

Spoon in hand, it taps the beats,

Dancing while it cooks and heats.

Chopping veggies, stirring sauce,

Singing loud, no need to gloss.

Call me a chef or disco king,

Cooking with music makes me swing.

Salad Struggles

Tried some greens, gave them a chew,

Tasted like the backyard dew.

Tossed in nuts and Cran delight,

Now this bowl puts up a fight.

Health can hide in leaves and lime,

One bite closer every time.

Bake-Off Battle

Flour flies and eggs go rogue,

Mixer's stuck in sugar mode.

Cakes deflate like sad balloons,

Cookies hard as lunchroom spoons.

Still I bake with hopeful beat,

Even flops are fun to eat.

CHAPTER 7

LIFE LESSONS WITH LAUGHTER

A heartfelt blend of wisdom and humor, these rhymes turn everyday experiences into joyful lessons.

Celebrating the bumps and breakthroughs of life, this section reminds us that laughter is often the best teacher.

Patience Practice

Waiting in line, time moves slow,

People groan and start to blow.

I smile calmly, but inside I'm mad,

Wishing I were anywhere but here, sad.

Patience is golden, or so they say,

Till hangry strikes and runs away.

The To-Do List Lie

Made my list, all neat and fine,

Crossed off tasks, felt so divine.

But new things pop up all the time,

The list grows long like a nursery rhyme.

Try your best, don't stress or cry,

Some days, "done" just means "don't try."

The Power Nap

Fifteen minutes, just a blink,

Wake up thinking, "What did I drink?"

Mind resets, then off I go,

Until I nap for hours, oh no!

Power naps can save your day,

Unless you sleep your life away.

Smile It Forward

Smile at strangers, make their day,

Unless they look like they might stay.

Kindness spreads like coffee stains,

Brightening moods and sometimes brains.

Life's a puzzle, grin and say,

"Here's a smile, now go away!"

Traffic Tango

Red lights dance as I proceed,

Patience is tested, slow speed.

Horn honks join the urban song,

But rushing never rights the wrong.

Can't teleport? Then here's your cue,

Sing out loud, and vibe the view.

CHAPTER 8

MISCELLANEOUS MISHAPS

A playful collection of everyday blunders and unexpected moments that catch us off guard.

From minor slip-ups to funny faux pas, these rhymes celebrate the imperfect and often hilarious side of life.

The Weather Wish

Checked the forecast, rain or shine,

Dressed for the sun, then caught the brine.

Umbrella left back at home,

Wet and cold, I walk and roam.

Life's weather can change fast,

Adapt, laugh, and make it last.

Fitness Fail

Started jogging, feeling proud,

Five minutes later, lost in the cloud.

Wheezing loudly, red as a beet,

Exercise? More like defeat!

Try again, but take it slow,

Maybe yoga? Yeah, let's go.

The Birthday Blunder

Forgot a friend's big day, oh no!

Quick message sent, hope it'll show.

Better late than never! true,

Friendship's strong when love shines through.

Life gets wild, our brains misplace,

Good friends still smile face-to-face.

Phone Battery Blues

Ninety percent, then fifty,

Then it drops down oh so swiftly.

Charger hunt becomes a quest,

"10% left!" Now I'm stressed.

Keep it charged, don't be caught,

In today's world, powers are sought.

CHAPTER 9

EVERYDAY JOYS

A celebration of life's simple pleasures, quiet moments, kind gestures, and unexpected smiles.

These rhymes capture the beauty found in the ordinary, reminding us that happiness often lives in the little things.

Cozy Corners

A comfy chair, a book, some tea,

Five minutes till someone yells for me.

I sit, I sip, I turn a page,

Then hear a crash, I disengage.

Still, these moments, short but gold,

This is how the tired soul is rolled.

Pet Antics

Dog zooms by like he's on fire,

Cat knocks cups, pure chaos, sire.

Hair on socks, the couch, my toast,

Guess who rules this house the most?

They fart, they bark, they steal your shoe.

But life's more fun with petting too.

84

Music Mornings

Songs that play to start my day,

Dance around, then head my way.

Music lifts the heaviest mood,

Tunes that make the day feel good.

Off-key? Yes. But vibes are strong,

Life's a jam, so sing it wrong.

Weekend Plans

No alarms, no rush, just rest,

Plans to do what suits me best.

Laundry? Nope. That's Monday's fight,

Today I nap and snack just right.

Weekend goals? Avoid all stress.

Pants optional. Success? Yes.

Coffee Cheers

A steamy cup, my daily hug,

First sip hits my brain, goes zugg.

Friends and chats over a brew,

Time to pause and just be you.

Spilled a bit? That's fine, I'm tough,

Caffeine makes me just enough.

Evening Calm

After chaos, peace descends,

Moments when the noise all ends.

Cuddle close or read a book,

Time to slow down, take a look.

Rest and love in gentle rhyme,

Family's treasure, endless time.

CHAPTER 10

TRAVEL & ADVENTURE

Rhymes that take you on a journey beyond the familiar, exploring new places, meeting new faces, and embracing the thrill of the unknown.

From road trips to wild escapades, these poems celebrate the spirit of adventure and discovery.

Packing Panic

Suitcase stuffed, or so I thought,

Forgot my shoes, oops! What a plot.

Shirts are wrinkled, pants are tight,

Will this trip survive the night?

Next time I'll pack with more care,

Or just wear pajamas everywhere.

Airport Shuffle

Lines and scans and trays to clear,
Announcements blare into your ear.
Announcements scream, "Gates moved again!"
I'm running like a frantic hen.
Travel's chaos, but don't pout,
Adventure's what it's all about.

Lost in Maps

GPS says, "Turn right now."
But roads don't match, oh, holy cow!
Spinning 'round like a confused top,
Asking strangers, "Hey, where's the shop?"
Getting lost? It's half the thrill,
Sometimes wrong leads right to chill.

Hotel Hideaway

Room key lost, no Wi-Fi nearby,

Mini bar's empty, oh dear! Bye-bye!

Snacks are missing, vanished thin.

Room service is slower than a snail on a spin.

Laugh through quirks and travel perks,

Strange decor and oddball clerks.

Souvenir Surprise

Bought a gift, a trinket small,

Packed it up with care for all.

Arrived home to find it broke,

Travel tales in every joke.

Souvenirs may break or go,

But funny stories steal the show.

Travel Buddy Troubles

Friend's playlist? A crime to ears,

Boy band hits for three whole years.

They sing off-key, ignore the map,

We stop for cheese and roadside crap.

Road trips test your friendship glue,

Survive the ride, you're bonded true.

Jet Lag Jam

Body clock? A busted joke,

Woke at dawn, my brain still broke.

Eyes like zombies, hair on tilt,

Dreams of sleep wrapped up in a quilt.

Jet lag hits like ninja sneezes,

Nap, then coffee! Pray it eases.

Tourist Trap

Souvenir shops are on every street,

Prices are high, and crowds repeat.

Bought a hat, fluorescent flair,

Blinded birds and scared a bear.

Traps or treasures? Who's to say?

It's all great content anyway.

Keychain Catastrophe

Souvenir signs scream, "Buy now!"

Caught up in it, don't ask how.

Five keychains, one odd fridge magnet,

None from places that I've tagged yet.

Still, they sparkle on display,

Proof I traveled in some way.

Shrunken Shirt Surprise

Bought a t-shirt that screamed "PARIS LIFE,"

Wore it once, then met the strife.

Washed it once, now much too small,

Shrunk so tight, I can't move at all.

Still, I wear it, bold and proud,

Fashion's pain just draws a crowd.

Language Blunder

Tried to say "bonjour" with flair,
Came out like I'd swallowed a chair.
Locals laughed, but it was sweet,
Gestures saved me on that street.
Language fails? C'est la vie!
Miming works universally.

Adventure Calls

Hiking hills or getting lost,

Blisters form, was it worth the cost?

Took a shortcut, found a goat,

Tripped and tossed my water coat.

Still, I grin and snap a pic,

Travel's weird, but magic sticks.

Street Food Struggles

Street food sizzles, smells divine,

Tried one bite, now I need nine.

Spicy mystery wrapped in dough,

My stomach said, proceed with no,

Still, I'd eat it all again

Travel diets never win.

Chapter 11

Friendships & Social Life

From heart-to-hearts to laugh-out-loud moments, this section celebrates the bonds that brighten our days.

These rhymes explore the joy, support, and occasional silliness that come with true friendship and vibrant social connections.

Textpectation

Waiting for that *ding!* No sound.

Two hours in, I'm message-bound.

Did they ghost me? Did they nap?

Checked my phone, then Google Maps.

Still, I wait with calm dismay,

True friends just reply, "Okay."

Party Fumble

Showed up early, feeling fine,

Then realized it's a wine-and-dine.

Clutched my juice, a lonely pour,

Suddenly, I'm fun no more.

Next time I'll bring a cheeky flask,

Blend in better, have a blast.

Social Media Scroll

Endless scroll through feeds galore,

Friends on beaches, drinks, and more.

Compare your life, then feel so small,

But remember: posts don't tell all.

Live your story, not the feed,

True friends know the heart you need.

Awkward Meet-Cute

Saw a friend I hadn't met,

Nervous words and eyes that fret.

Do I know you? Maybe not,

Moments lost that time forgot.

Laugh it off, no harm done,

Friendships start with silly fun.

Group Chat Chaos

Buzz, buzz, buzz! It just won't end,

Fifty memes from just one friend.

Typing gone, then back again,

Is this chat or psychic pain?

Still, I smile, though slightly dazed,

Love in chaos, emoji-laced.

Plan? What Plan?

Made a plan, then vanished quick,

Mood just changed, classic trick.

Friends forgive, they understand,

Life's not always what we planned.

Friends just laugh, they know the game,

Plans may flop, but love's the same.

The Compliment Trap

You look great! I flash a grin,

Friend says, "Ugh, don't look at my chin."

We all see flaws that no one spots,

Worrying over phantom dots.

So toss out praise like its confetti,

Confidence makes folks feel ready.

Support Squad

Friend calls up, the drama's real,

Bad day vibes and a missing meal.

I nod and "mm-hmm" like a pro,

Sometimes that's all you need to show.

No advice, no grand big speech,

Just snacks and hugs within arm's reach.

The Forgetful Friend

Birthday bash, balloons on cue,

One friend ghosted, where were you?!

Life gets busy, days collide,

Friendship's not a ticking tide.

Send a meme, then laugh some more,

They'll show up late, with cake galore.

Coffee Date Clumsy

Spilled my drink, oh! what a splash!

Laughed so hard, forgot the crash.

Friends forgive my messy ways,

We cherish those imperfect days.

Life's a mess, but laughs unfold,

With friends around, it's pure gold.

\- END -

© 2025 Rey Sañosa. All rights reserved.

www.ingramcontent.com/pod-product-compliance
Lightning Source LLC
Chambersburg PA
CBHW030942310726

48969CB00008B/2342